COOKBOOK

Sonia Mansata is a high school teacher. She is also passionately fond of cooking. She specializes in Italian, Continental and Chinese dishes and in designer chocolates. She runs her own catering service.

Sonia lives in Kolkata with her husband and two daughters.

COOKBOOK

Sonia Mansata

PUFFIN BOOKS

PUFFIN BOOKS

Penguin Books India (P) Ltd., 11 Community Centre, Panchsheel Park, New Delhi 110017, India

Penguin Books Ltd., 80 Strand, London WC2R 0RL, UK

Penguin Group Inc., 375 Hudson Street, New York, NY 10014, USA

Penguin Books Australia Ltd., 250 Camberwell Road, Camberwell, Victoria 3124, Australia

Penguin Books Canada Ltd., 10 Alcorn Avenue, Suite 300, Toronto, Ontario M4V 3B2, Canada

Penguin Books (NZ) Ltd., Cnr Rosedale & Airborne Roads, Albany, Auckland, New Zealand

Penguin Books (South Africa) (Pty) Ltd., 24 Sturdee Avenue, Rosebank 2196, South Africa

First published in Puffin by Penguin Books India 2003

Text copyright © Sonia Mansata 2003

Illustrations copyright © Penguin Books India 2003

10 9 8 7 6 5 4 3 2 1

Illustrations by Sudeepa Ghosh

This book is dedicated to my daughters Abhilasha and Aashna since it was written keeping them in mind. And to my husband Ashok for his unstinting support.

Typeset in AGaramond by Eleven Arts, Delhi-35

Printed at International Print-O-Pac, Noida

CONTENTS

CAKES, BISCUITS AND TARTS

DESSERTS

TIPS FOR YOUNG CHEFS

- Before you start cooking, read the whole recipe.
- Make sure you have all the ingredients ready.
- Measure all ingredients carefully.
- Have all the equipment (e.g. knife, bowl, measuring cup, etc.) you will require handy.
- Make sure you have understood all the cooking terms (e.g. sauté, roast, grill, etc.) used in the recipe. Refer to the section under the 'commonly used cooking terms'.
- Once you have mastered a particular recipe, feel free to add your own touches to it. A good chef always innovates.
- Always wear an apron for protection while you are cooking.
- Have a hand towel ready for wiping your hands.
- Use oven gloves to protect your hands whenever you pick up hot utensils or when putting things into the oven or taking them out. It is recommended that you ask an adult for help.
- When using a knife hold it carefully, with the sharp edge pointing downwards. Always use a chopping board for cutting the ingredients.
- Whenever you need to stir food while cooking, use

a wooden spoon and keep the pan steady by holding the handle firmly.

- Make sure your hands are dry before you operate any electric gadgets like ovens, toasters, etc.
- Do not lose heart in case your first attempt is not a success. Cooking is a skill you gradually acquire. Try again and you will succeed.

Tips for Using a Mixer-blender

- Place the mixer-blender at a convenient height so that you can use it without having to stretch.
- It is recommended that you ask an adult to help you to use the mixer-blender.
- Use the appropriate blades for the work at hand, e.g. dry grinding, wet grinding, whipping etc.
- Never run a mixer-blender with an empty jar.
- Always use a spatula to do any necessary scraping inside a jar, for the blades are often sharp.
- Make sure that the jar is properly closed before you switch on the mixer-blender.
- Switch off the mixer-blender and wait for the blades to stop rotating before you open the lid of the jar.
- When you finish using the mixer-blender switch off the source of power. Wash the jars and blades immediately. Dry well and store.

Tips for Using a Microwave Oven

- It is recommended that you ask an adult for help in operating the microwave oven.

- Never use metal dishes or containers for microwave cooking. Glass is suitable. Special ceramic containers meant for microwave cooking are also available.

- In case you need to cover the dish use a glass or ceramic plate. Don't use aluminium foil which is used in a conventional oven.

- Don't try to open the door while the microwave activity is going on in the oven.

- Pierce any food that has a skin, while cooking, such as tomatoes, grapes, etc.

- Don't use any vessel or dishes with metal parts.

- In case there is any sparking while cooking, immediately turn off the power.

- In a microwave oven the cooking process continues even after the oven has been switched off, so allow the food to remain in the oven for a few minutes after switching off the oven.

- Never operate a microwave oven when it is empty.

- Don't use printed paper napkins or plastic bags for microwave heating as the dye from the printing can transfer to the food.

Tips for Using an Oven or OTG

- It is recommended that you ask an adult for help when using the oven.
- Set the oven temperature correctly.
- Always pre-heat the oven so that it has reached the correct temperature before putting the food inside.
- Use oven gloves while handling hot dishes.
- Make sure the dishes you use for baking are ovenproof.

Tips for Using a Pressure Cooker

- It is essential that you ask an adult for help when using a pressure cooker.
- You must know the correct way to fit the lid into the cooker body and to remove it.
- Never fill your cooker more than $2/3$ full, otherwise the vent pipe may get blocked. That can be dangerous.
- Take care that the pressure cooker is on a level cooking surface.
- Never remove the gasket while the lid is hot.
- Never use your pressure cooker without water.
- Vent tube and safety valve must always be clear of all residues.

- Place the ingredients in the cooker, close it and put it over high heat. When the steam comes out of the valve in a steady stream, cover it with the weight. Be very careful not to burn yourself with the steam.

- Wait for the first whistle which shows that the cooker has reached full pressure. Lower the heat, note the time and keep the cooker on low heat for the time given in the recipe.

- When your cooking is done allow the cooker to cool and reach room temperature before you open the lid. You can also allow cold tap water to run over the cooker if you wish to save time.

- Use soapy water to clean the cooker. Always dry the cooker before storing it.

- Don't close the cooker when storing it, as this may cause unpleasant odours.

Tips on Steaming

- Steaming is one of the healthiest forms of cooking and is done in a special utensil called a steamer. It consists of two pans that fit tightly on top of each other, and has a tight-fitting lid. Water is boiled in the lower pan and the food to be steamed is put in the upper one, which has a perforated base, for the steam to come through.

- If you don't have a steamer, you can make one yourself. Take a large pan which has a tight-fitting lid. Place a metal bowl, large enough to hold the food to be steamed, in the pan. Pour water into the pan so that it comes half way up the bowl.
- Boil the water and place the food in the bowl. Cover the pan and steam the food over boiling water for the time given in the recipe.
- It is recommended that you ask an adult for help when steaming.

Tips on Grating Chocolate or Cheese

- The best way to grate chocolate or cheese is to first chill it for about an hour until it is firm.
- Grate the chocolate or cheese with a grater which has medium to large holes. You can keep the grated items in a container covered with a tight-fitting lid in the freezer until you need it.

How to Make Roasted Cumin Powder

- Roasted cumin powder, when sprinkled over salads and snacks gives a nice tangy taste to the dish.
- Heat a non-stick pan over low heat. Put 1 tbsp of whole cumin seeds in it and roast it, stirring all the while, for 4-5 minutes, until the cumin turn brown. You can ask an adult for help.

- Remove the pan from the heat and let the cumin cool.

- Crush it to powder with a rolling pin.

- Store it in an airtight container until required.

How to Make Perfect Pasta/Noodles

- Any type of pasta or noodles should be cooked al dente—with a bite. This means it should be tender, but firm, and the strands should be separate. Remember that pasta continues to cook even after you have removed it from the heat, so take it off just before it is ready. Pasta should always be served hot, so make sure that the sauce and all accompaniments are ready in advance. Cook the pasta just before serving it. Soggy, overcooked or cold pasta tastes terrible.

- Always cook pasta in a large, deep pan with plenty of boiling salted water. Fill the pan two-thirds with water. Add 1 tsp salt and a few drops of refined oil to it. Put the pan over high heat and bring it to boil. You can ask an adult for help.

- Add the pasta and let it cook for the time given on the packet.

- Pick up a strand with a fork and bite it to test if it is done.

- Drain the pasta in a colander and run cold water

over it. Return it to the pan and put it over low heat to allow the water to evaporate and to heat through.

■ Serve immediately.

How to Prepare a Smooth White Sauce

■ White or béchamel sauce is a basic and very useful sauce to learn. It is used in many dishes and is really quite easy to prepare. It is made with butter, flour and milk, and seasoned with salt, pepper and whatever else the recipe calls for. Use the quantities given in the recipe you are following.

■ Melt the butter over low heat in a small pan. Add the flour and keep stirring it with a flat-based, wooden spoon, if possible, till it starts sizzling. Make sure it does not turn brown. Keep scraping the sides and base of the pan to prevent it from sticking.

■ Remove the pan from the heat and wait for the sizzling to stop. Pour in the milk at one go and stir vigorously to remove all lumps. Always use cool or lukewarm milk. Adding hot milk will turn the sauce lumpy.

■ Return the pan to medium heat and cook, stirring all the while, until the sauce thickens. Season according to the recipe and carry on.

■ If the sauce does get lumpy, don't worry—just strain it through a strainer.

■ If you prepare the sauce in advance, it will cool and develop a skin on the top. Then when you stir the sauce it will get lumpy and all your efforts will go to waste. To avoid the skin forming, put a piece of butter paper over the entire surface of the sauce, so that it is touching the surface.

How to Make a Light Shortcrust Pastry

■ Shortcrust pastry is used to make tarts, flans and a variety of other baked biscuits, etc.

■ It is made with butter, flour and water along with other seasonings or flavourings that are called for in the recipe. Use the ingredients and quantities given in the recipe.

■ Sift the flour with all the dry ingredients together into a bowl.

■ Add cold butter to it and cut it into the flour with two knives.

■ Lightly rub the butter into the flour with your fingerprints until the mixture resembles breadcrumbs. Raise your hands while doing this, so that the air gets introduced into the pastry and makes it light.

■ Sprinkle in cold water, a little at a time and mix it gently and quickly to form a firm dough, which is not sticky and does not have cracks in it.

- Put the pastry back into the bowl, cover it with cling film and keep it in the refrigerator for 30 minutes.

More About Pastry

How to line tartlet tins with pastry

- Lightly grease the tartlet tins.
- Roll out the chilled pastry with the help of a little flour, and cut it into circles slightly larger than the tartlet tins.
- Place a circle of pastry over a tartlet tin and gently press it with your fingers to line the tin. Trim off any excess pastry along the edges with a knife.

How to bake blind

- Sometimes, when making tarts, we need to bake the pastry before filling it. In this case, we need to ensure that the pastry does not puff up. This is done by baking blind.
- Line the tartlet tin with pastry and prick it evenly with a fork.
- Place a piece of foil over the pastry and fill it with dry beans.
- Bake for the time specified in the recipe.
- Remove the tins from the oven, let them cool on a wire rack and slide out the pastry cases.

FIRST AID

A first aid kit is a must in every home.

A basic first aid kit should contain:

- Antiseptic lotion
- Antiseptic ointment
- Cotton wool
- Plaster
- Band-aid
- Ointment for burns and scalding
- Bandages

In Case of Minor Cuts

- Clean the cut with cotton and antiseptic lotion.
- If bleeding does not stop, apply ice to the cut.
- Apply antiseptic ointment and Band-aid.
- Change the dressing regularly until the cut heals.

In Case of Minor Burns or Scaldings

- Soak the affected area in a bowl of ice-water.
- Clean with antiseptic lotion.
- Apply ointment for burns gently.
- Bandage loosely.

WEIGHT AND VOLUME

Flour

1 tbsp (heaped)	= 10 gms
1 cup	= 100 gms

Sugar

1 tbsp (heaped)	= 30 gms
1 cup	= 175 gms

Water

1 cup	= 160 ml

Baking powder

1 tsp	= 5 gms

Abbreviations

tbsp	tablespoon
tsp	teaspoon
ml	millilitre
gm	grams

TOOLS

Knife
for cutting &
chopping

Tablespoon
for stirring &
measuring

Teaspoon
for stirring &
measuring

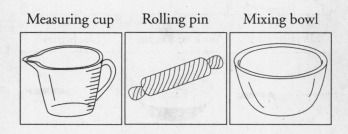

Measuring cup

Rolling pin

Mixing bowl

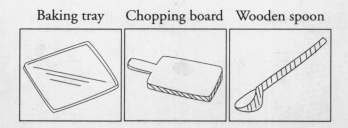

Baking tray

Chopping board

Wooden spoon

Oven Mitts
to protect your
hands while handling hot
utensils during baking

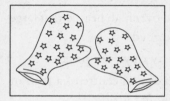

Slotted Spoon
ideal for deep frying
as it allows the oil to
drain away

Kitchen Scales
help to measure individual
ingredients accurately

OTG
oven cum toster
cum grill

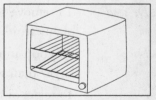

COOKING TERMS

Blend	To combine ingredients to a smooth paste in a blender.
Boil	To cook liquid over high heat so that large bubbles are formed.
Chop	To cut into very tiny even pieces.
Core	To remove seeds and centre of a fruit or vegetable without cutting it.
Cube	To cut into small even square pieces.
Deep fry	To cook over high heat using plenty of oil. A deep frying pan or wok may be used.
De-seed	To remove seeds and surrounding pulp of any fruit or vegetable.
Dice	To chop into tiny even pieces, slightly larger than when you chop.
Discard	To reject or throw away.
Drain	To remove liquid from the solid portions.
Fold	To mix gently with a large metal spoon, using a figure-of-eight motion.
Garnish	To add finishing touches to make the dish look more appealing. Chopped herbs or grated cheese are often used as garnishes.
Grease	To apply a thin layer of butter or oil to a dish to prevent food sticking to it.

Grill	To apply dry heat to a dish from above to cook and brown e.g. gratins.
Marinate	Mostly used for fish and meat. When we smear fish or meat with sauces, herbs or spices, and allow them to rest for at least 30 minutes in order to tenderize and allow the flavours to penetrate.
Mash	To break up larger pieces by using pressure to form a smooth paste. A potato masher is ideal.
Mince	To cut into extremely tiny pieces, smaller than when you chop.
Peel	To remove the peel or outer covering. A peeler is often used for this.
Pre-heat	To heat the oven to the required temperature before baking.
Sauté	To cook over high heat, stirring briskly. A wok or kadhai is suitable.
Shallow-fry	To fry in a frying pan using little oil. A non-stick frying pan is ideal for this.
Shred	To tear with your hands into long thin pieces, generally with cooked meat.
Sift	To pass flour and other dry ingredients through a sieve. It removes unwanted particles and allows air to be introduced into the flour.

Simmer	To cook a liquid over moderate heat so that gentle bubbles are formed.
Soft boil	Usually refers to eggs. Eggs which are cooked in simmering water for 6 minutes so that the white is firmly set but the centre of the yolk is still soft and dark yellow.
Stock	Liquid in which vegetables, fish or meat have been cooked. This often is used in soups and sauces.
Strain	To pass liquid through a strainer to remove suspended particles.

GLOSSARY

Almond	badam
Apple	seb
Cabbage	band gobi
Capsicum	Shimla mirch
Carrot	gaajar
Cashew nut	kaju
Cinnamon	dal chini
Cauliflower	phool gobi
Corriander leaves	hara dhania
Cottage cheese	paneer
Cumin	jeera
Curd	dahi
Flour	maida
Green peas	mattar
Nutmeg	jaiphal
Parsley	ajmood
Pistachio	pista
Prawns	jhinga
Spinach	palak
Sultana	kishmish
Walnut	akhrot
Wholemeal flour	atta

SYMBOLS

The following symbols have been used:

 To indicate vegetarian version of a non-vegetarian dish.

 To indicate that this step may be hazardous. You should proceed with caution and adult supervision is recommended for younger children.

 To indicate that this should only be done under adult supervision.

Safety

While cooking can be great fun, it is important to be careful. It is recommended that you have an adult helping you when you are cooking on the stove, or using the oven, microwave or blender, or using a sharp knife. It is essential that you have an adult helping you when you are using a pressure cooker.

Drinks – Hot and Cold

Chocolate Soda

Summer Cooler

Lassi

Hot Chocolate

Strawberry Milkshake

CHOCOLATE SODA

SERVES—6

Ingredients

Cocoa powder – 2 tbsp
Icing sugar – 200 gms
Cornflour – 2 tsp
Vanilla ice-cream – 6 scoops
Soda – 6 bottles (500 ml each)

Equipment

Deep pan with handle
Wooden spoon
Ice-cream scoop or
    tablespoon
Tall glasses

Mix the cocoa powder and icing sugar together in a deep pan. Stir in 1 cup of water and heat gently till well mixed.

Mix the cornflour with 1 tbsp of water and add to the cocoa mixture. Cook stirring constantly till the sauce thickens.

Put one scoop of ice-cream into each tall glass. Top with chocolate sauce and soda. Serve at once.

You can make any soda of your choice by changing the sauce. Strawberry or pineapple syrup could be used instead of chocolate sauce.

SUMMER COOLER

SERVES—2

Ingredients

Lime juice – 2 tbsp
Vanilla ice-cream – 2 scoops
Lemon squash – 4 tbsp
Sprite/7-Up – 1 bottle (500 ml)

Equipment

Blender
Ice-cream scoop or
    tablespoon
Glasses

Put the lime juice, vanilla ice-cream, lemon squash and $1/2$ cup of water in the blender. Blend till smooth.

Top with Sprite/7-Up.

Pour into glasses and serve chilled.

Pour some prepared lemon squash and chopped mint leaves into ice trays and freeze. Top the above drink with these ice cubes.

LASSI
SERVES—2

Ingredients
Curd – 1 cup
Sugar – 1¹/₂ tbsp
Milk – 1 cup (cold)
Rose syrup – 1 tbsp
Ice cubes – 6 cubes

Equipment
Blender
Spoons
Glasses

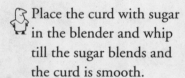

Place the curd with sugar in the blender and whip till the sugar blends and the curd is smooth.

Add the cold milk, rose syrup and ice-cubes. Whip till well blended and frothy.

Pour into glasses and serve.

Lassi is supposed to cool the system during the summer months. Instead of rose syrup you can use any syrup of your choice e.g. pineapple or mango.

HOT CHOCOLATE

SERVES—1

Ingredients

Milk – 1 glass
Sugar to taste
Cocoa powder – 1 tsp
Drinking chocolate – 2 tsp
Cinnamon powder – $1/4$ tsp
Grated chocolate – 1 tsp (see p. xiv)

Equipment

Deep thick-based pan
Tall mug
Spoon

Heat the milk with sugar in a deep pan over low heat till the sugar melts and the milk is hot.

In a tall mug mix cocoa and drinking chocolate together. Add 1 tsp of the hot milk to the chocolate and mix till a smooth and thick paste forms. There should be no lumps.

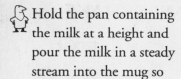Hold the pan containing the milk at a height and pour the milk in a steady stream into the mug so that a foam forms.

Sprinkle the cinnamon powder and grated chocolate over the hot chocolate and serve at once.

STRAWBERRY MILKSHAKE

Ingredients

Fresh, ripe strawberries – 8
Sugar – 1 tbsp
Vanilla ice–cream – 1 cup
Milk – 1 glass (chilled)
Ice cubes – 6–8

Equipment

Chopping board
Knife
Blender
Tablespoon
Tall glass

Wash and clean the strawberries.

Slice each strawberry into 5–6 slices. Sprinkle sliced strawberries with sugar and set aside till a dark pink syrup forms.

Place strawberries (except 2 slices), syrup and ice-cream in the blender and blend till smooth.

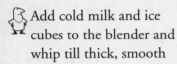 Add cold milk and ice cubes to the blender and whip till thick, smooth and frosty.

Pour into a pretty tall glass. Decorate with remaining strawberry slices and serve.

You can make mango or pineapple milkshake by using sliced mango or pineapple.

Soups and Salads

Simple Gazpacho

Baby Corn and Mushroom Soup with Pasta

Chicken Noodle Soup

Fishball and Vegetable Soup

Green Pea Soup

Mixed Bean Salad

Russian Salad

Macaroni and Cucumber Salad

Fruity Tuna Salad

Aloo Chaat

SIMPLE GAZPACHO

SERVES—6

Ingredients

Tomato juice – 1 litre
Garlic – 2 cloves (crushed)
Sugar – 2 tbsp
Pepper powder – $1/2$ tsp
Salt – 2 tsp
Cucumbers – 2
Tomatoes – 3
Onions – 2
Capsicum – 1
Bread – 4 slices
Oil – 5 tbsp

Equipment

Blender
Large strainer
Chopping board
Vegetable peeler
Knife
Small bowls
Soup bowls

Place the tomato juice with garlic, sugar, pepper and salt in the blender and blend well.

Strain the juice into a ceramic or glass container and chill.

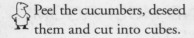 Peel the cucumbers, deseed them and cut into cubes.

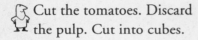 Cut the tomatoes. Discard the pulp. Cut into cubes.

Cut the onions and capsicum into cubes.

Remove the crusts from the bread slices and discard them. Cut the bread slices into small squares. Heat the oil in a frying pan and fry a few pieces at a time till brown and crisp. Keep them in an airtight container.

Serve the cold tomato soup with the cubed vegetables and fried bread as accompaniments, for each guest to add according to their own taste.

This is a delightfully refreshing soup to serve during the hot summer months.

BABY CORN AND MUSHROOM SOUP WITH PASTA

SERVES—6

Ingredients

Olive oil – 2 tbsp
Fresh mushrooms – 200 gms
  (sliced)
Salt – 1 tsp
Pepper to taste
Onion – 1 (chopped)
Garlic – 4 cloves (chopped)
Vegetable or chicken stock –
  6 cups
Baby corn – 200 gms (sliced)
Milk – 1 cup
Mozzarella or any cooking cheese
  – 1/2 cup
Pasta (macaroni,
  (fusilli or penne) – 1/2 cup

Equipment

Chopping board
Knife
Frying pan
Bowls
Deep pan
Ladle
Soup bowls

Heat 1 tbsp olive oil in a
frying pan. Sauté the
mushrooms with salt and
pepper till the mushrooms
begin to brown slightly.
Keep aside.

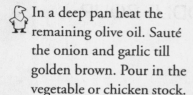 In a deep pan heat the remaining olive oil. Sauté the onion and garlic till golden brown. Pour in the vegetable or chicken stock.

Add the sliced baby corn and sautéed mushrooms. Mix in the milk. Adjust seasoning. Stir in the cooking cheese. Cook over low heat till the cheese melts. Cook the pasta as described on p. xv and add it to the soup.

If the soup becomes too thick add a little more stock.

Spoon soup into soup bowls and serve hot.

Chopped parsley can be sprinkled over each bowl of soup.

CHICKEN NOODLE SOUP

SERVES—6

Ingredients

Chicken – 500 gms
Onion – 1 (peeled)
Ginger – 1" piece (peeled)
Peppercorns – 4
Salt – 1 tsp
Carrot – 1 (sliced thin)
Cabbage – a few leaves (sliced thin)
Spinach – 250 gms (whole leaves)
Capsicum – 1/2 (sliced thin)
Water – 6 cups
Noodles – 1 small packet (50 gms)

Equipment

Pressure cooker
Vegetable peeler
Large strainer
Chopping board
Knife
Deep pan
Medium pan
Ladle
Soup bowls

 Put the cleaned, cut and washed chicken with the whole onion and ginger into the pressure cooker. Add the peppercorns, salt and water, and pressure cook for 6 minutes.

 Remove chicken pieces from the cooker. Leave to cool a bit. Shred the chicken and discard the bones.

Strain the stock into a deep pan and keep aside. Discard the onion, ginger and peppercorns.

 Cook the carrot slices for a few minutes in $1/2$ cup of salted water. Drain and keep aside.

 Cook the noodles as given on p. xv.

 Reheat the stock with the shredded chicken. Add the vegetables and heat for 3 minutes.

Place some boiled noodles in the soup bowls and pour the hot soup over it.

Serve this soup piping hot with soya sauce, chilli sauce and green chillies soaked in vinegar if you like.

FISHBALL AND VEGETABLE SOUP

SERVES—6

Ingredients

Boneless white fish (beckti, mackerel or plaice)– 250 gms
Prawns (cleaned) – 200 gms
Egg – 1
Oil – 1 tsp
Parsley – 1 sprig (chopped)
Salt – 1 tsp
Pepper – 1/4 tsp
Ginger – 2" piece (peeled)
Onion – 1 (peeled)
Peppercorns – 5
Cabbage – a few leaves (shredded fine)
Spinach – 1/2 bunch (shredded fine)
Lettuce – 1/4 bunch (shredded fine)

Equipment

Mixer-blender
Deep pan with lid
Slotted spoon
Strainer
Ladle
Soup bowls

Mince the raw fish with the prawns in the mixer. Add upto 1 tbsp of water if necessary to obtain a paste.

Add the egg, oil, parsley, salt and pepper. Mix well.

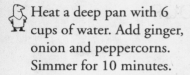 Heat a deep pan with 6 cups of water. Add ginger, onion and peppercorns. Simmer for 10 minutes.

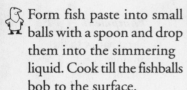 Form fish paste into small balls with a spoon and drop them into the simmering liquid. Cook till the fishballs bob to the surface.

Remove cooked fishballs with a slotted spoon and repeat the process till all of the fish paste is used.

Remove from heat and strain the liquid. Reheat. Add fishballs. Add the vegetables. Add salt and pepper to taste.

Pour into soup bowls with a ladle.

Serve steaming hot.

You can add your favourite vegetables if you like. Parboil the vegetables and add along with the others.

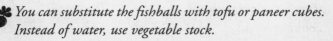 *You can substitute the fishballs with tofu or paneer cubes. Instead of water, use vegetable stock.*

GREEN PEA SOUP

SERVES—6

Ingredients

Shelled green peas – 500 gms
Peppercorns – 6
Ginger – 2″ piece (peeled)
Butter – 50 gms
Flour – 3 tbsp
Milk – 2 cups
Salt – 1 tsp

Equipment

Deep pan with lid
Strainer
Blender
Deep pan
Ladle
Soup bowls

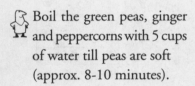 Boil the green peas, ginger and peppercorns with 5 cups of water till peas are soft (approx. 8-10 minutes).

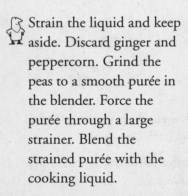 Strain the liquid and keep aside. Discard ginger and peppercorn. Grind the peas to a smooth purée in the blender. Force the purée through a large strainer. Blend the strained purée with the cooking liquid.

Use the butter, flour and milk to prepare the white sauce as given on p. xvi.

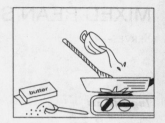

 Heat green pea purée. Stir in the sauce. Add salt to taste. Heat through.

Spoon soup into soup bowls with a ladle and serve with hot, buttered toast.

MIXED BEAN SALAD

SERVES—6

Ingredients

Chana – $1/4$ cup
Rajma – $1/4$ cup
Sprouted moong beans –
  $1/2$ cup
Cucumber – 1 (cubed)
Tomato – 1 (cubed)
Onion – 1 (chopped fine)
Coriander leaves – 1 bunch
  (chopped fine)
Juice of 1 lime
Roasted cumin powder – $1/2$ tsp (see p. xiv)
Green chilli – 1 (chopped) (optional)
Salt – 1 tsp

Equipment

Bowls
Pressure cooker
Strainer
Big mixing bowl
Chopping board
Knife
Big spoon
Lemon squeeze

Soak chana and rajma
separately overnight.
Drain.

 Add 1 cup of water to each
and pressure-cook for 25
minutes. Drain and cool.

Mix sprouted moong beans, boiled chana and boiled rajma together.

Add cucumber, tomato, onion and coriander leaves. Toss to mix well.

Add roasted cumin powder, lemon juice and salt to taste. Mix well and serve cold.

RUSSIAN SALAD

SERVES—4

Ingredients

French beans – 8-10
Carrots – 2
Potatoes – 2 (medium)
Shelled green peas – 150 gms
Capsicum – 1
Salt – as required
Eggs – 3
Mayonnaise – 1 cup
Cream – $1/2$ cup
Sugar – 1 tbsp
Lettuce – a few leaves

Equipment

Chopping board
Knife
Vegetable peeler
Deep pan
Bowl for mixing
Spoon
Salad bowl

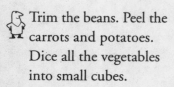 Trim the beans. Peel the carrots and potatoes. Dice all the vegetables into small cubes.

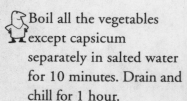 Boil all the vegetables except capsicum separately in salted water for 10 minutes. Drain and chill for 1 hour.

Boil the eggs for 8 minutes. Shell. Slice neatly.

Mix the mayonnaise, cream and sugar together. Chill for 1 hour.

Mix the boiled vegetables, capsicum and mayonnaise-cream mixture together. Adjust seasoning.

Line a salad bowl with the lettuce leaves. Spoon the salad into the salad bowl. Decorate with the sliced boiled eggs. Serve cold.

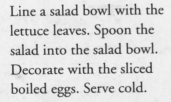

MACARONI AND CUCUMBER SALAD

SERVES—4

Ingredients

Macaroni – 1 cup
Salt – as required
Cucumber – 2
Thick fresh curd – 1 1/2 cups
Fresh cream – 1/2 cup
Oil – 1 tsp
Green chilli – 1 (chopped)
Mustard seeds – 1/4 tsp
Curry leaves – a few

Equipment

Deep pan
Colander
Chopping board
Vegetable peeler
Knife
Strainer
Big spoon
Big bowl
Small pan
Egg beater

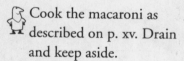 Cook the macaroni as described on p. xv. Drain and keep aside.

Peel the cucumbers. De-seed and cut into small cubes, and keep aside.

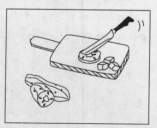

Place the curd in a strainer lined with a thin muslin cloth, over a bowl, and leave the whey to drain out for 30-45 minutes.

Beat the curd with fresh cream. Add the cucumber cubes and macaroni. Add 1 tsp salt and mix well.

Heat the oil in a small pan and add the green chilli, mustard seeds and curry leaves. Fry for 2-3 minutes till mustard seeds stop sputtering. Add to the curd-macaroni salad. Mix well. Chill for 1 hour and serve cold.

FRUITY TUNA SALAD

SERVES—4

Ingredients

Tuna – 200 gms (tinned)
Apple – 1
Pineapple bits – $1/2$ cup
Orange – 1 (segmented)
Castor sugar – 1 tbsp
Juice of $1/2$ lime
Lettuce – a few leaves
Grapes – 200 gms
Walnuts – 2 tbsp (chopped)
Sultanas (kishmish) – 2 tbsp
Mayonnaise – 1 cup
Salt to taste

Equipment

Chopping board
Knife
Big bowl
Salad bowl

Flake the tuna into thick flakes.

Chop the apple (with its skin), pineapple bits and orange segments into equal-sized pieces.

Mix in the sugar and lime juice. Chill for 1 hour.

Shred half the lettuce. Use
the bigger leaves to line
the salad bowl.

Mix the chopped fruits,
grapes, walnuts, sultanas,
and shredded lettuce
lightly. Add the
mayonnaise and mix till
mayonnaise coats the
salad.

Gently mix in the tuna.
Chill for 1 hour. Serve
cold.

ALOO CHAAT

SERVES—6

Ingredients

Potatoes – 6 (big)
Tamarind paste – 1 tbsp
Jaggery – 250 gms (grated)
Ginger – 1 tbsp (shredded)
Salt – 1$\frac{1}{2}$ tsp
Curd – 2 cups
Chaat masala – 1$\frac{1}{2}$ tsp
Roasted cumin powder – 1 tsp
    (see p. xiv)
Chilli powder – $\frac{1}{2}$ tsp (optional)
Black salt – 1 tsp
Sev – 6 tbsp
Coriander leaves – 2 tbsp (chopped)

Equipment

Pressure cooker
Grater
Knife
Deep pan
Bowl
Egg beater
Quarter plates

Pressure-cook potatoes for 6 minutes. till cooked. Allow to cool. Peel and cut into round slices.

Mix tamarind paste with $\frac{1}{2}$ cup of water in a deep pan. Add the jaggery. Stir and cook over low heat for 5 minutes to melt the jaggery.

Add the ginger and simmer
for 10 minutes. Remove
from heat and cool.

Add the salt to the curd in
a bowl and beat with an
egg beater till smooth.

Arrange the potato slices
on 6 quarter plates.
Sprinkle chaat maala,
roasted cumin powder,
chilli powder (if used) and
black salt equally over the
potato slices.

Divide the beaten curd
between the six plates and
spread over the potato slices.

Drizzle tamarind chutney
over the curd. Garnish
with sev. and coriander
leaves, and serve at once.

*If readymade papdis are easily available, you can
spread a few papdis on each plate before you arrange
the potato slices and you can make papdi-chaat. Chaat
tastes lovely if the curd and chutney are cold.*

Bread Delights

Open Tuna Sandwich

Egg-mayonnaise Sandwich

Grilled Ham, Tomato and Cheese Sandwich

Chicken Salad Submarine

Cheesy Garlic Pinwheels

Chicken Burger

Vegetable Cheese Hotgang

Sloppy Joes

Quick Pizza

OPEN TUNA SANDWICH

SERVES—4

Ingredients

Bread – 4 large slices
Butter to spread
Lettuce – a few leaves
Tuna – 100 gms (tinned, with oil)
Cream – 2 tbsp
Parsley – 1 tbsp (chopped fine)
Salt – $1/2$ tsp
Pepper to taste
Olives – a few (sliced thin)
Capsicum – $1/2$ (cut into triangles)
Tomato – $1/2$ (pulp removed and
    cut into thin, long slices)

Equipment

A round cutter
Chopping board
Knife
Small bowls
A fork
A plate for serving

Use a round bowl or cutter to cut the slices of bread into circles.

Spread butter over the bread circles.

Shred the lettuce leaves. Place them on the upper half of each bread circle. They should stick out a bit.

Mix the tuna along with the oil, cream, parsley, salt and pepper. Mash well till you have a smooth paste.

Spread the above paste over the bread circles thickly. Don't cover the lettuce completely.

Place 2 olive slices on each bread circle to form eyes. Use a capsicum triangle for a nose and a tomato strip for a smiling mouth.

These sandwiches are very easy to make and look very attractive.

EGG-MAYONNAISE SANDWICH

SERVES—2

Ingredients

Eggs – 4
Mayonnaise – $1/2$ cup
Tomato ketchup – 4 tbsp
Parsley – 1 tbsp (chopped fine)
Salt – $1/4$ tsp
White bread – 4 slices
Brown bread – 4 slices

Equipment

Deep pan
Bowl
Potato masher
Star-shaped
  cookie cutter
Chopping board

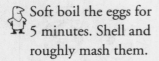 Soft boil the eggs for 5 minutes. Shell and roughly mash them.

Mix in the mayonnaise, ketchup, parsley and salt.

Use a cookie cutter to cut stars from the bread slices.

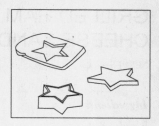

Spread the white bread stars with a generous helping of egg mayonnaise.

Top with brown bread stars. Serve with chips or French fries.

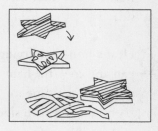

If you don't have a cookie cutter you could make the sandwiches into triangles or squares.

GRILLED HAM, TOMATO AND CHEESE SANDWICH

SERVES—4

Ingredients

Bread – 8 slices
Butter to spread
Ham – 4 slices
Tomatoes – 2 (sliced)
Cheese slices – 4
Pepper to taste
Salt – $1/4$ tsp
Onion – 1 (sliced) (optional)
Capsicum – $1/2$ (cut into strips) (optional)

Equipment

A non-stick frying pan
An OTG or toaster
Chopping board
Knife
Plate

Butter bread slices on one side.

 Heat a non-stick frying pan and cook the ham slices one at a time for $1/2$ minute on each side.

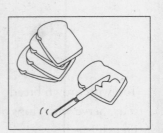

Place cooked ham slices on the unbuttered side of four slices of bread.

Top the ham slices with tomato slices. If you like

you can add onion and capsicum slices along with the tomato slices at this stage.

Cover with cheese slices.

Finally place the remaining four slices of bread with the buttered side on top.

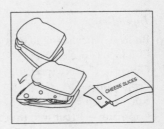

 Grill the sandwiches under the griller till the top is golden brown. Then turn the sandwiches over so that the underside can also brown. By this time the cheese slices should have melted.

Cut the grilled sandwiches into triangles and serve hot with potato wafers and tomato ketchup.

The sandwiches can also be cooked in a sandwich toaster.

CHICKEN SALAD SUBMARINE

SERVES—1

Ingredients

Boneless chicken – 250 gms
Onion – 1 (peeled)
Ginger – 1″ piece (peeled)
Peppercorns – 5
Salt – $1/2$ tsp
Capsicum – 1 (cut into thin
    strips)
Tomato – 1 (pulp removed
    and cut into thin strips)
Celery – 1 tbsp
    (chopped fine)
Mayonnaise or thousand
    island dressing – $1/2$ cup
Milk bread – 1 loaf
Butter to spread
Pepper to taste
Lettuce – a few leaves

Equipment

Deep pan
Chopping board
Knife
Spoon
Plate

Cook the washed chicken with the onion, ginger, peppercorns, salt and $1/2$ cup water over low heat till tender.

Let the chicken cool, and cut it into thin strips. Mix

with tomato, capsicum
and celery.

Mix in the mayonnaise or
thousand island dressing.

Cut the milk bread in half
horizontally. Apply butter
on the cut sides. Sprinkle
with salt and pepper.

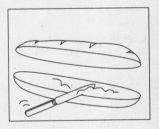

Place the lettuce leaves
over the lower portion of
the loaf. Pile chicken salad
on top. Cover with the
upper portion.

Use toothpicks to hold
the submarine together.

Serve with potato wafers.

 *Corn niblets and sautéed mushrooms can be used
instead of chicken to make a vegetarian submarine. You
can also use eggless mayonnaise which is readily
available in the market.*

CHEESY GARLIC PINWHEELS

SERVES—6

Ingredients

Garlic – 6-8 cloves
Mayonnaise – 1/2 cup
Bread – 6 large slices (crusts
    removed)
Cheese spread – 6 tbsp

Equipment

Steamer
Rolling pin
Bowl
Knife
Big plate
Cling film

Crush the garlic cloves.
Mix them with the
mayonnaise.

Steam each of the bread
slices for 10-15 seconds
(see p. xiii–xiv).

Gently roll the slices with a rolling pin to flatten them slightly.

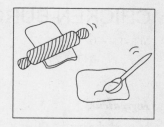

Spread each slice with 1 tbsp of cheese spread.

Spread the mayonnaise-garlic mix over the cheese spread. Roll the bread slices. Wrap the bread rolls in cling film and chill for 1 hour.

Cut the rolls into 3-4 slices and serve.

 You can use eggless mayonnaise which is available in the market.

CHICKEN BURGER

SERVES—6

Ingredients

Minced chicken – 500 gms
Onion – 1 (chopped fine)
Garlic – 5 cloves (chopped fine)
Parsley – 2 tbsp (chopped fine)
Salt – 1 tsp
Peeper – $1/2$ tsp
Egg – 1
Oil – 3 tbsp
Onions – 3 (sliced)
Buns – 6
Butter to spread
Lettuce – a few leaves
Tomatoes – 3 (sliced)
Capsicum – 3 (sliced)

Equipment

Chopping board
Knife
Mixer-blender
Bowl
Non-stick frying pan
Spatula
Toothpicks
Plate

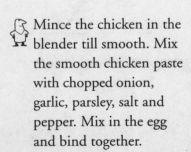 Mince the chicken in the blender till smooth. Mix the smooth chicken paste with chopped onion, garlic, parsley, salt and pepper. Mix in the egg and bind together.

Shape the chicken paste into six patties.

 Heat the oil in a non-stick frying pan and shallow fry the chicken patties till cooked (approx. 10 minutes). Drain and keep aside.

 Sauté the onion slices in the same pan till soft.

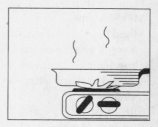

Cut the buns in half horizontally. Butter the cut sides. Place lettuce leaves on the lower half of the buns.

Place tomato and capsicum slices on top of the lettuce leaves. Place chicken patties on the tomato and capsicum slices.

Top with onion slices and place the upper halves of the buns on top. Use toothpicks to hold the burgers together.

VEGETABLE CHEESE HOTGANG

SᴇʀᴠᴇS—6

Ingredients

Butter – 100 gms
Flour – 3 tbsp
Milk – 2 cups
Mixed vegetables (French beans,
carrots, green peas, cauliflower,
capsicum) – 2 cups (diced,
boiled in salted water and
drained)
Salt – 1 tsp
Pepper to taste
Cheese – 100 gms (grated)
Hot dog rolls or buns – 6

Equipment

Chopping board
Knife
Deep pan
Non-stick frying pan
Spoon
Grater
OTG
Plate

Use 50 gms of the butter,
the flour and milk to
prepare the white sauce as
described on p. xvi-xvii.

Add the boiled mixed
vegetables and mix well.
Add salt and pepper.

Stir in half the grated
cheese. Cook over low
heat for a few more
minutes. Remove from
heat and cool.

Cut a thin lid from the
hot dog rolls or buns.
Scoop out the inside of
the rolls leaving a narrow
rim all around.

Butter the inside of the
scooped out rolls.

Fill with the cooled
vegetable mixture.

Sprinkle the remaining
grated cheese over the
vegetable-filled rolls.

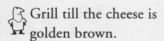

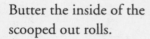 Grill till the cheese is
golden brown.

Serve hot.

SLOPPY JOES

SERVES—6

Ingredients

Chicken mince – 400 gms
Oil – 3 tbsp
Onions – 2 (sliced)
Garlic – 6 cloves (chopped)
Salt – 1 tsp
Pepper – $1/2$ tsp
Flour – 2 tbsp
Tomato purée – 100 gms
Sugar – 1 tbsp
Buns – 6
Butter to spread

Equipment

Bowl
Strainer
Deep pan
Spoon
Knife
Baking tray
Grill
Plates

Wash the mince and drain
well, using a strainer.

Heat the oil in a pan. Add
the onions and garlic. Fry
till golden.

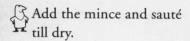 Add the mince and sauté till dry.

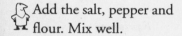 Add the salt, pepper and flour. Mix well.

Mix in tomato purée and sugar with 1 cup of water.

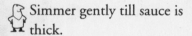 Simmer gently till sauce is thick.

Halve the buns and spread the cut sides with butter. Grill till golden brown.

Serve toasted buns with the mince sauce poured on top.

You could garnish the Sloppy Joes with grated cheese.

QUICK PIZZA
SERVES—6

Ingredients

Tomato purée – 1 cup
Tomato ketchup – 2 tbsp
Sugar – 1 tbsp
Salt – 1 tsp + 1 tsp
Pepper to taste
Garlic – 4 cloves (crushed)
Oregano – $1/2$ tsp
Flour – 250 gms
Baking powder – 1 tsp
Butter – 50 gms
Milk – 7–8 tbsp
Tomatoes – 2 sliced
Capsicum – $1/2$ sliced
Mozzarella or any cooking
    cheese – 200 gms (grated)

Equipment

Deep pan
Spoon
Knife
Big bowl
Rolling pin
Baking tray
Grater
Oven

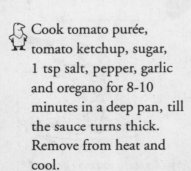 Cook tomato purée,
tomato ketchup, sugar,
1 tsp salt, pepper, garlic
and oregano for 8-10
minutes in a deep pan, till
the sauce turns thick.
Remove from heat and
cool.

Use the flour, baking powder, 1 tsp salt, butter and milk (instead of water) to prepare the pastry dough as described on p. xvi.

Divide the dough into 6 balls. Roll each ball into a circle. Lay circles of dough on a greased baking tray.

Spread tomato sauce over them. Leave a narrow margin along the edge.

Arrange the tomato and capsicum slices on top.

Sprinkle grated cheese and bake till cheese melts and is slightly coloured.

You can use any topping of your choice.

Meal-in-a-Dish

Fisherman's Pie

Spinach Loaf

Quiche Lorriane

Creamy Pasta

Chicken Tetrazinni

Garlic-fried Chicken with Crispy Potatoes

Cheese and Potato Bake

Noodles with Shrimp and Vegetable Sauce

Simple Khow Swey

FISHERMAN'S PIE

SERVES—4

Ingredients

Boneless white fish – 250 gms
  (cubed)
Prawns (cleaned) – 250 gms
Onion – 1 (peeled)
Parsley – 1 sprig + 1 tbsp
  (chopped)
Butter – 3 tbsp + 3 tbsp
Flour – 3 tbsp
Milk – 1 cup + $\frac{1}{2}$ cup
Potatoes – 5 medium (boiled
  and peeled)
Salt – 1 tsp + 1 tsp
Pepper – $\frac{1}{4}$ tsp + $\frac{1}{4}$ tsp

Equipment

Deep pans
Slotted spoon
Strainer
Big bowl
Potato masher
Fork
Baking dish
OTG

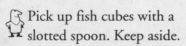 Boil the fish in $1\frac{1}{2}$ cups of water with the whole onion and parsley sprig in a deep pan for 5 minutes.

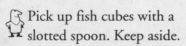 Pick up fish cubes with a slotted spoon. Keep aside.

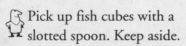 In the same liquid cook prawns till they turn pink. Don't overcook the prawns.

Remove prawns. Strain stock and keep aside.

 Use 3 tbsp butter, 3 tbsp flour, 1 cup milk and the stock to prepare the white sauce as described on p. xvi-xvii. Season it with 1 tsp salt and 1/4 tsp pepper. Add the chopped parsley.

Mix fish and prawns. Pour into a baking dish.

Mash potatoes. Add 3 tbsp butter, 1 tsp salt and 1/4 tsp pepper. Gradually add 1/2 cup milk and mash till smooth and creamy. Spread the marked potatoes over the prawn and fish mixture.

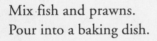

 Grill till brown. Serve hot.

 For a vegetarian pie, use 200 gms of boiled cauliflower florets, 100 gms of boiled peas and 100 gms of tinned mushrooms in place of fish and prawns.

SPINACH LOAF

SERVES—6

Ingredients

Oil – 2 tbsp
Onions – 2 (sliced fine)
Garlic – 4 cloves (crushed)
Spinach – 500 gms.
  (chopped fine)
Tomatoes – 2 (chopped fine)
Cottage cheese/paneer –
  200 gms (grated)
Salt – 2 tsp
Flour – 1 tbsp
Double cream – 200 ml
Eggs – 5
Nutmeg powder – $1/4$ tsp
Cheese – 50 gms (grated)

Equipment

Non-stick pan
Spoon
Knife
Chopping board
Grater
Baking dish
OTG

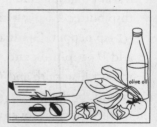

Heat the oil in a non-stick pan. Add the onions and garlic, and sauté till golden. Add the spinach and tomatoes.

Stir and cook over high heat till dry. Add the paneer and mix well. Add 1 tsp salt.

Mix flour into the cream. Stir well to ensure that there are no lumps.

 Add to the spinach mixture. Stir well and cook for a few minutes.

Remove from heat and cool.

Beat the eggs with salt and nutmeg powder. Mix into the cool spinach mixture.

Pour the mixture into a baking dish. Sprinkle with grated cheese.

 Preheat the oven to 200°C. Bake for 25 minutes or till a knife inserted in the centre comes out clean.

Serve hot.

QUICHE LORRIANE

SERVES—4

Ingredients

Flour – 125 gms
Butter – 60 gms
Bacon – 150 gms
Eggs – 3
Cream – 500 ml
Salt – 1/2 tsp
Pepper to taste
Capsicum – 1/2 (sliced)
Cheese – 100 gms (grated)

Equipment

Big bowls
Chopping board
Knife
Non-stick pan
Rolling pin
Tartlet tins (four to six)
Aluminium foil
Dry beans
Plate for serving

Use the flour and butter
to prepare the pastry as
described on p. xvii. Chill

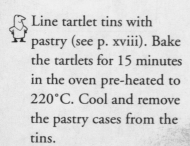 Line tartlet tins with
pastry (see p. xviii). Bake
the tartlets for 15 minutes
in the oven pre-heated to
220°C. Cool and remove
the pastry cases from the
tins.

Chop bacon into cubes and sauté in a non-stick pan till it is crisp.

Beat eggs, cream, salt and pepper together in a bowl.

Divide the sautéed bacon among pastry cases. Top with capsicum slices. Pour the egg mixture over this. Sprinkle the grated cheese on top.

 Place the tartlets on a baking tray. Bake for 25 minutes or till the filling is firm in the oven pre-heated to 180°C.

The bacon can be omitted. Chopped and sautéed spinach or sliced and sautéed mushrooms could be used instead.

Serve as individual quiches or cut into wedges.

CREAMY PASTA

SERVES—4

Ingredients

Spaghetti or fettucini – 200 gms
Salt – 1/2 tsp + 1 tsp
Oil – 1/2 tsp + 2 tbsp
Ham – 100 gms
Eggs – 2
Cream – 1/2 cup
Pepper – 1/2 tsp
Grated cheese – 3 tbsp

Equipment

Sauce pans
Colander
Frying pan
Wooden spoon
Bowl
Grater
Dinner plates

Cook the pasta as described on p. xv, using 1/2 tsp salt and oil.

Chop ham into small pieces. Heat 2 tbsp of oil in a frying pan and sauté till light brown.

Beat the eggs and cream together. Add 1 tsp salt and pepper.

 In a saucepan mix the pasta, cream and ham together. Heat gently tossing to coat the pasta with the sauce. Cook over gentle heat for 5 minutes.

Spoon onto plates. Sprinkle with grated cheese and serve.

You could use tomato or spinach pasta to make this dish more colourful.

You can omit the ham. Use 50 gms of corn niblets and 50 gms of boiled green peas instead.

CHICKEN TETRAZINNI

SERVES—4

Ingredients

Chicken – 500 gms
Onion – 1 (peeled)
Ginger – 1" piece (peeled)
Salt – 1 tsp
Butter – 50 gms
Flour – 2 tbsp
Milk – 2 cups
Pepper – $1/2$ tsp
Spaghetti – 1 cup (boiled see p. xv)
Parsley – 2 tbsp (chopped fine)
Cheese – 60 gms (grated)

Equipment

Deep pan
Strainer
Knife
Chopping board
Non-stick deep pan
Baking dish
OTG

 Boil chicken with onion, ginger, a little salt and 1 cup of water for 20 minutes.

Cool, then shred the chicken and discard the bones.

Strain the stock and keep aside. Discard the onion and ginger.

 Use the butter, flour, milk and stock to prepare the white sauce as described on p. xvi.

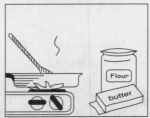

Add the salt and pepper.

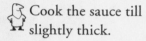 Cook the sauce till slightly thick.

Remove from heat. Add the shredded chicken, boiled spaghetti and chopped parsley. Mix well.

Pour into a baking dish. Sprinkle the grated cheese on top and bake in an oven pre-heated to 220°C for 15 minutes.

Then grill till cheese turns golden brown.

 You can omit the chicken. Use 2 cups of mixed, diced and boiled vegetables (beans, carrots, peas and cauliflower).

While making the sauce use 2$\frac{1}{2}$ cups of milk in place of stock.

GARLIC-FRIED CHICKEN WITH CRISPY POTATOES

SERVES—4

Ingredients

Chicken with bones – 1 kg
  (cut into small pieces)
Garlic – 8 cloves (crushed)
Juice of 1 lime
Salt – 1 tsp + $1/2$ tsp + $1/2$ tsp
Pepper – $1/2$ tsp + $1/4$ tsp + $1/4$ tsp
Flour – $1/2$ cup
Egg – 1 (lightly beaten)
Cornflour – $1/2$ cup
Chopped parsley – 1 tbsp
Oil for frying
Potatoes – 4 (boiled and peeled)
Wholemeal flour (atta) – 1 cup

Equipment

Deep frying pan
Bowls
Spoon
Plate

Wash the chicken pieces and marinate them with the crushed garlic, lime juice, 1 tsp salt and $1/2$ tsp pepper for 1 hour.

In a deep bowl mix the flour and cornflour. Add $1/2$ tsp salt, $1/4$ tsp pepper and the parsley to it. Beat in the egg and enough water to make a thick batter.

Heat the oil in a deep frying pan. Take the chicken pieces from the marinade and dip them in the batter. Fry 2-3 pieces at a time over low heat till the chicken is cooked and the batter turns golden brown.

Drain the chicken well. Repeat with the remaining chicken.

Cut the boiled potatoes into thick fingers. Season wholemeal flour with ¹/₂ tsp salt and ¹/₄ tsp pepper. Coat potato fingers with it. Fry them in the same oil till crisp.

Serve fried chicken with crispy fried potatoes and tomato ketchup.

 Cubes of paneer (400 gms) could be used instead of chicken.

CHEESE AND POTATO BAKE

SERVES—4

Ingredients

Boiled potatoes – 8 (peeled
    and cut into rounds)
Onions – 4 (cut into rounds)
Salt – $1/2$ tsp
Pepper – $1/2$ tsp
Mozzarella or cooking cheese –
    200 gms
Cream – 500 ml

Equipment

Knife
Grater
Deep baking dish
Spoon
OTG

Take a deep baking dish
and grease it. Line it with a
layer of boiled potatoes.

Then spread a layer of
onions. Season with salt
and pepper.

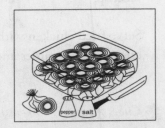

Sprinkle with cheese.

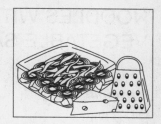

Repeat layers. Finish with
a layer of potatoes.

Pour cream over the layers.

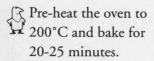 Pre-heat the oven to
200°C and bake for
20-25 minutes.

Serve hot.

 Potato lovers will relish this simple yet delicious dish.

NOODLES WITH SHRIMP AND VEGETABLE SAUCE

Ingredients

Oil – 2 tbsp
Onion – 1 (sliced)
Cauliflower – few pieces
Carrot – 1 (cut into thin strips)
Cabbage – 200 gms (sliced)
Spinach – 200 gms (sliced)
Soy sauce – 1 tsp
Vinegar – 1 tsp
Salt – 1 tsp
Shrimps – 200 gms (cleaned)
Cornflour – 2 tbsp
Noodles – 100 gms

Equipment

Pan
Colander
Frying pan
Spoon
Knife
Plate

In a pan, heat the oil. Add the sliced onion and sauté till soft. Add the cauliflower and carrot. Sauté for 5 minutes. Add the remaining vegetables, soy sauce, vinegar and salt. Sauté for 2 minutes.

Add 1/2 cup of water and the shrimps. Cook till shrimps turn pink.

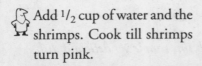

Mix the cornflour to a
paste with a little water
and add to the vegetables.
Cook till thick. Remove
from heat.

Don't overcook the
vegetables and shrimps.

 Boil the noodles as
described on p. xv.

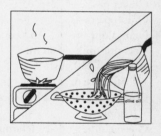

In a plate spread the
noodles. Top with shrimp
and vegetable sauce.

*You can garnish with chopped spring onions on top if you
like.*

 *You can use 100 gms of tofu cut into fingers instead of
shrimps.*

SIMPLE KHOW SWEY

SERVES—4

Ingredients

Chicken – 1 kg (cut into pieces)
Salt – 1 tsp
Oil – 3 tbsp + $1/2$ cup
Garlic paste – $1^1/2$ tbsp
Ginger paste – 1 tbsp
Onion paste – 2 tbsp
Gram flour (besan) – 3 tbsp
Coconut milk – 500 ml
Noodles – 200 gms
   (boiled see p. xv)
Coriander leaves – 2 bunches
   (chopped)
Green chillies – 8–10 (chopped)
Onions – 3 (chopped)
Lime – 3 (cut into pieces)

Equipment

Deep pans
Large strainer
Frying pan
Wooden spoon
Small bowls
Soup bowls

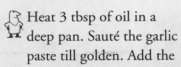 Boil the chicken with salt and 5 cup of water till done. Shred the chicken and discard bones. Reserve stock.

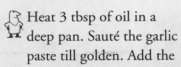 Heat 3 tbsp of oil in a deep pan. Sauté the garlic paste till golden. Add the

ginger and onion pastes. Sauté till oil separates.

Stir in the gram flour and sauté for 4 minutes. Add the chicken, stock and coconut milk.

Add salt to taste. If necessary add 2 cups of water. Simmer the khow swey for 20 minutes.

In a frying pan heat $1/2$ cup of oil. Fry half the boiled noodles a little at a time till golden. Drain and store in an airtight container.

Serve the khow swey with boiled and fried noodles in separate bowls. In small bowls serve the coriander leaves, chillies, onions and lime for the guests to help themselves.

You can use diced, boiled, mixed vegetables in place of chicken.

Cakes, Biscuits and Tarts

Lemon Tart

Apple Pie

Creamy Corn Tarts

Chocolate-covered Animal Cookies

Gingerbread Men

Fairy Cakes

Easy Chocolate Cake

Chococrunch

LEMON TARTS
SERVES—4

Ingredients
Butter – 50 gms + 100 gms
Flour – 100 gms
Icing sugar – 50 gms + 150 gms
Egg – 1 (lightly beaten)
Custard powder – 2 tbsp
Lime or lemon juice – 2 tbsp

Equipment
Sieve
Mixing bowl
Knives
Pan
Wooden spoon
Tartlet tins
Fork
Aluminium foil
Dry beans
OTG

Mix 50 gms of butter into the flour as described on p. xvi.

Add 50 gms of icing sugar and knead lightly into a dough using the beaten egg. Add a little cold water if needed. Chill the dough for 30 minutes.

Heat 1 cup of water. Stir in 150 gms icing sugar. Stir till sugar dissolves. Add the custard powder mixed with a little water and cook stirring constantly till thick. Add lime or lemon juice and remove from heat.

Mix in 100 gms of softened butter and set the lemon curd to refrigerate.

Roll the dough and prepare the tartlet tins for baking blind as described on p. xvii.

 Bake in a pre-heated oven at 180°C for 15-20 minutes.

Remove tartlets from cases. Cool. Fill with chilled lemon curd.

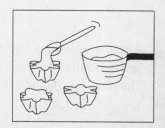

APPLE PIE

SERVES—4

Ingredients

Apples – 4 (peeled and sliced)
Juice of 2 oranges ($^1/_2$ cup)
Sugar – 6 tbsp
Sultanas (kishmish)– 1$^1/_2$ tbsp
Cinnamon powder – $^1/_2$ tsp
Flour – 200 gms
Butter – 100 gms + 1 tbsp
Icing sugar

Equipment

Deep pan
Bowls
Spoon
Pie dish
Rolling pin
Knife
OTG

 Cook the apples, orange juice, sugar and sultanas together in a deep pan over low heat till the liquid dries up. Mix in cinnamon powder.

Use the flour and 100 gms of butter to prepare the pastry as described on p. xvii, and chill it.

Grease the pie dish. Roll the dough with the help of a little flour into a large circle. Line the pie dish with it. Trim off excess pastry.

Fill the pie dish with the apple filling. Roll the excess pastry and cut into strips. Lay pasty strips in a criss-cross pattern over the apple filling. Use a little water to fix pastry strips to the edges.

Pre-heat the oven to 200°C. Bake the pie for 20 minutes. Take out and brush with 1 tbsp butter. Bake again for 5-10 minutes till pale gold. Dust with icing sugar and serve.

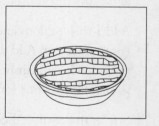

Apple pie tastes great with a scoop of vanilla ice-cream.

CREAMY CORN TARTS

SERVES—4

Ingredients

Butter – 2 tbsp + 100 gms
Onion – 1 (sliced)
Capsicum – $1/2$ (sliced)
Flour – 1 tbsp + 200 gms
Milk – 1 cup
Cream-style corn – 200 gms
Salt and pepper to taste
Cheese – 100 gms (grated)
Tomato ketchup – to decorate

Equipment

Frying pan
Wooden spoon
Bowl
Rolling pin
Tartlet tins
Aluminium foil
Dry beans
Grater
Plate

Heat 2 tbsp of butter in a frying pan. Sauté onion and capsicum till soft.

Add 1 tbsp of flour and continue to stir. Add the milk slowly and stir briskly so that lumps don't form.

Stir in the corn and cook the mixture till thick Add the salt and pepper.

Remove from heat and cool.

Use 200 gms of flour and 100 gms of butter to make the pastry as described on p. xvii. Chill the pastry and prepare the tartlet tins for baking blind as described on p. xviii.

 Bake in the oven pre-heated to 220°C for 20 minutes. Cool and remove beans and foil. Remove pastry cases from tins.

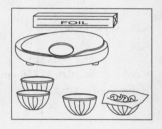

Fill the pastry cases with the corn mixture. Sprinkle generously with grated cheese.

 Grill till the cheese melts and turns golden brown.

Decorate with a dot of ketchup. Serve hot.

CHOCOLATE-COVERED ANIMAL COOKIES

SERVES—6 TO 8

Ingredients

Butter – 100 gms
Flour – 175 gms
Baking powder – 1 tsp
Icing sugar – 100 gms
Egg yolk – 1
Vanilla essence – 1/2 tsp
Cooking chocolate – 250 gms
Refined oil – 1 tsp

Equipment

Sieve
Bowl
Rolling pin
Animal-shaped cookie
    cutters
Baking trays
Wire rack
Non-stick pan
Saucepan
Spoon
Butter paper
Fancy foil paper

Mix the butter into the flour, baking powder and icing sugar as described on p. xvii.

Add the egg yolk and vanilla essence and knead to a smooth dough. If necessary add 1 tsp of milk.

Chill the dough for 30 minutes.

 Pre-heat the oven to 200° C.

With the help of a little flour roll out the dough utill quite thin. Use animal-shaped cookie cutters to cut out cookies. Dip the cutters in flour so that they don't stick to the dough.

Place the cookies on a greased baking tray. Gather remaining dough, roll again and cut more cookies.

Bake the cookies for 15-20 minutes or till golden brown. Cool on a wire rack.

Put the cooking chocolate in a non-stick pan over a pan or bowl of hot water till it has melted. Add 1 tsp of oil to it. Mix well.

Dip cookies one by one in the melted chocolate and place on trays covered with butter paper. Chill for 1 hour. Wrap in fancy paper and refrigerate till needed.

GINGERBREAD MEN

SERVES—6

Ingredients

Butter – 100 gms
Brown sugar – 175 gms
Honey – 4 tbsp
Flour – 300 gms
Ginger powder – 2 tsp
Soda bicarbonate – 1 tsp
Egg – 1
Sultanas (kishmish) – a few

Equipment

Pan
Seive
Bowl
Wooden spoon
Rolling pin
Gingebread biscuit cutters
Baking tray
Wire rack

Set the oven to 190°C.

Put butter, sugar and honey in a pan and stir them together over low heat till melted.

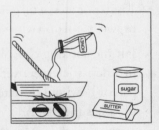

Sift the flour, ginger powder and soda bicarbonate into a bowl.

Add the honey-butter
mixture and egg.

Mix everything together
and knead into a ball.

Chill for 30 minutes.

With the help of a little
flour roll the dough till
quite thin. Using biscuit
cutters cut out the shapes
of gingerbread men. Dip
the cutters in flour so
that they don't stick to the
dough. Place biscuits on a
greased baking tray.

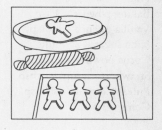

Gather up remaining
dough. Roll it out and
cut more shapes.

Use the sultanas to create
eyes and buttons for the
gingerbread men.

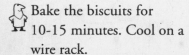 Bake the biscuits for
10-15 minutes. Cool on a
wire rack.

FAIRY CAKES

SERVES—6

Ingredients

Butter – 125 gms
Castor sugar – 125 gms
Eggs – 2
Flour – 125 gms
Baking powder – 1 tsp
Vanilla essence – $1/2$ tsp
Icing sugar – 250 gms
Cocoa powder – 2 tbsp
Strawberry syrup – 1 tbsp
Pineapple syrup – 1 tbsp
Gems – 10-15

Equipment

OTG
Deep bowl
Wooden spoon
Sieve
Paper sweet cases
Baking tray
Spoon
Bowls
Knife

Set the oven to 180°C.

Put the butter in a deep bowl. Beat with a wooden spoon till soft.

Add the sugar and beat together till light and creamy.

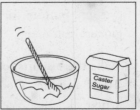

Add the eggs one at a time and beat well.

Sift the flour and the baking powder together. Add a little at a time to the egg-butter mixture. Fold in well. Mix in the vanilla essence.

 Spoon cake batter into paper sweet cases. Place paper sweet cases on a baking tray and bake for 10-15 minutes till cakes are firm and golden brown.

Cool them on a wire rack.

Sift icing sugar into a bowl and add enough water to make a thick paste. Divide into 3 bowls. Add cocoa powder, strawberry syrup and pineapple syrup to the different bowls.

Spread a little coloured icing on each cake with a knife and decorate with contrasting coloured Gems.

EASY CHOCOLATE CAKE

Ingredients

Flour – 100 gms
Cocoa – 4 tbsp
Baking powder – 1 tsp
Butter – 100 gms
Castor sugar – 60 gms
Eggs – 3
Vanilla essence – $1/2$ tsp
Milk – 2 tbsp

Equipment

Sieve
Deep bowl
Wooden spoon
Cake tin
Microwave oven or OTG
Wire rack

Sift flour, cocoa and
baking powder together.

Beat soft butter with sugar
in a deep bowl till fluffy.

Beat in eggs one at a time.

Gradually beat in flour
mixture. Beat till smooth.
Add essence. Mix well.
Stir in milk.

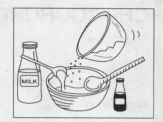

Grease the cake tin and
pour in the batter.

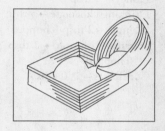

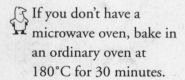 Microwave for 5 minutes.

If you don't have a
microwave oven, bake in
an ordinary oven at
180°C for 30 minutes.

Unmould on a wire rack
and let it cool.

Cut into slices and serve.

CHOCOCRUNCH

SERVES—6

Ingredients

Butter – 100 gms
Honey – 4 tbsp
Drinking chocolate – 5 tbsp
Walnuts – 2 tbsp (chopped)
Sultanas (kishmish) – 1 tbsp
    (chopped)
Cornflakes – 150 gms

Equipment

Pan
Wooden spoon
Paper sweet cases

 Mix butter and honey in a pan over low heat till the butter has melted. Stir in drinking chocolate. Remove from heat.

Stir chopped walnuts, sultanas and cornflakes to the above mixture. Let the mixture cool for 30 minutes in the pan.

Place a heap of the above mixture into each individual paper sweet case. Let it cool till it hardens and sets.

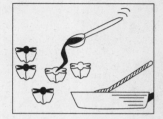

Desserts

Trifle

Mango Fool

Peach Melba

Apple crisp

Devil's Temptation (Chocolate Pie)

Citrus Snow

Ice-cream Sandwich with Fudge Sauce

Ice-cream Bon-bons

Fruity Bread Pudding

TRIFLE
SERVES—6

Ingredients

Sponge cakes slices – 250 gms
Mixed fruit jam
Tinned mixed fruit – 400 gms
Red crystal jelly – 100 gms
   (strawberry/rasberry)
Milk – 2 cups
Sugar – 3 tbsp
Custard powder – 1 tbsp
Almonds – a few
Cherries – a few

Equipment

Deep glass bowl
Knife
Colander
Pan
Spoon

Cut sponge cake into even slices. Use the mixed fruit jam to make sandwiches with the sponge cake. Line a deep glass bowl with these sandwiches cut into small pieces.

Drain the tinned fruit. Spread the fruit over the sponge cake layer.

Make the jelly according to the instructions on the packet. Cool.

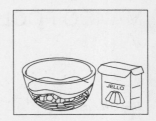

Pour over the fruit and cake layer. Place in the refrigerator for 6-8 hours till the jelly sets.

 In a pan, heat the milk and sugar together till the sugar dissolves. Mix the custard powder with a little water to make a smooth paste. Stir it into the milk. Cook till the custard thickens. Cool. Spread custard over the jelly.

Decorate with slivers of almonds and cherries. Serve cold.

MANGO FOOL

Serves—6

Ingredients

Milk – 2 cups
Sugar – 5 tbsp
Custard powder – 2 tbsp
Milk powder – 4 tbsp
Ripe, sweet mangoes – 6

Equipment

Pan
Spoon
Knife
Blender
Strainer
Big bowl

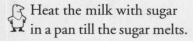 Heat the milk with sugar in a pan till the sugar melts.

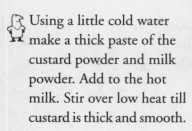 Using a little cold water make a thick paste of the custard powder and milk powder. Add to the hot milk. Stir over low heat till custard is thick and smooth.

Cool the custard and refrigerate for 2-3 hours.

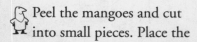 Peel the mangoes and cut into small pieces. Place the

mango pieces in the
blender and blend to form
a thick purée.

 Strain the mango purée.
Mix mango purée with
the cold custard. Whip in
the blender till smooth
and fluffy. Chill.

Serve cold.

*This is a real treat that you can prepare very easily during
the mango season.*

PEACH MELBA

Serves—6

Ingredients

Mixed fruit jam – 5 tbsp
Cornflour – 2 tbsp
Tinned peaches – 6 halves
Vanilla ice-cream – 6 scoops
Wafer biscuits

Equipment

Pan
Wooden spoon
Ice-cream bowls
Ice-cream scoop or
  tablespoon
Tea spoon

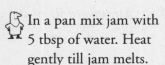 In a pan mix jam with 5 tbsp of water. Heat gently till jam melts.

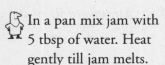 Mix the cornflour with a little water and add to jam sauce. The colour of the sauce will change. Cook over low heat stirring all the while till the sauce thickens and the original colour returns. This is the melba sauce. Chill.

In a pretty ice-cream
bowl, place a peach half.
Top with a scoop of
vanilla ice-cream.

Drizzle melba sauce over
the peach and ice-cream.
Serve at once with a
wafer biscuit.

APPLE CRISP
SERVES—6

Ingredients

Apples – 500 gms
Juice of 2 oranges – $1/2$ cup
Sugar – $1/2$ cup + $1/2$ cup
Marie or digestive biscuits
    (crumbled) – $1/2$ cup
Butter – 50 gms
Walnuts – 150 gms
Cinnamon powder – 1 tsp

Equipment

Peeler
Knife
Chopping board
Pan
Shallow baking dish
Bowl
OTG

Peel and core the
apples. Slice them
thinly.

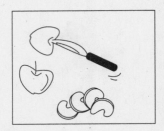

Cook the apples with
the orange juice and
$1/2$ cup sugar till soft
and pulpy.

Spread cooked apples in a shallow baking dish.

Mix biscuit crumbs, butter, walnuts, cinnamon and $1/2$ cup sugar together.

Sprinkle this mixture on top of the apples and bake for 25 minutes in the oven pre-heated to 180°C or till the top is crisp and golden.

Serve hot.

Apple crisp also tastes wonderful when served with a scoop of vanilla ice-cream.

DEVIL'S TEMPTATION (CHOCOLATE PIE)

SERVES—4

Ingredients

Marie biscuits – 200 gms
Butter – 50 gms + 50 gms
Castor sugar – 25 gms + 25 gms
Milk – $^1/_2$ cup
Cornflour – 1 tbsp
Cooking chocolate – 100
  gms (grated)

Equipment

Rolling pin
Pan
Pie dish
Heavy-based pan
Spoon

Crush biscuits, but not too fine.

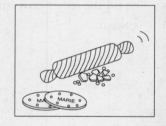

Melt 50 gms of butter in a pan. Mix in biscuit crumbs and 25 gms of sugar.

Use the above mixture to line a pie dish. Press the mixture onto the base and sides with the back of a spoon. Chill the crust for 30 minutes.

 To make the filling, heat 50 gms of butter, 25 gms of sugar and milk together in a heavy-bottomed pan. Add the cornflour mixed to a thick paste with water. Cook till the sauce thickens, stirring constantly.

Remove from heat. Add chocolate into hot sauce till it melts. Cool.

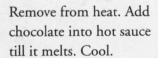

Fill prepared crust with the filling and chill.

Cut in wedges and serve.

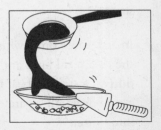

CITRUS SNOW

SERVES—6

Ingredients

Cystal jelly (orange) – 100 gms
Cream – $1/2$ cup
Egg whites – 2
Castor sugar – 3 tbsp

Equipment

Pan
Spoon
Bowl
Whisk
Egg beater

 In a pan make the orange jelly according to the instructions given on the packet but use only half the quantity of water specified.

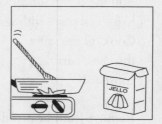

Cool the jelly and refrigerate till it begins to set.

In a separate bowl whisk the cream till light and fluffy. Don't over-beat the cream or it will separate into butter.

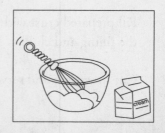

In another bowl whip the egg whites with an egg beater till fairly stiff. Add the sugar and whip till soft peaks form when the beater is lifted.

Stir the cream into the thickened jelly mixture.

Fold in the egg whites gently.

Refrigerate till the pudding sets.

ICE-CREAM SANDWICH WITH FUDGE SAUCE

Serves—6

Ingredients

Sponge cakes slices – 12 even
  pieces
Vanilla ice-cream – 6 slices
Condensed milk – 200 gms
Butter – 50 gms
Sugar – 2 tbsp
Cocoa powder – 6 tbsp

Equipment

Pan
Spoon
Knife
Aluminium foil
Plates

Take two slices of sponge
cake. Cut an even slice of
vanilla ice-cream.
Sandwich the ice-cream
slices between two slices
of cake.

Make 6 such ice-cream
and cake sandwiches.

Wrap each sandwich
separately in pieces of
foil. Freeze.

In a pan, heat condensed milk, butter, sugar and cocoa powder together till sauce turns thick and sticky.

To serve, take out a sandwich and unwrap. Cut each sandwich diagonally to form triangles.

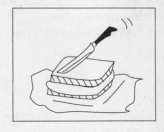

Serve the triangles with hot fudge sauce.

ICE-CREAM BON-BONS

SERVES—6

Ingredients

Vanilla ice-cream – 6 cups
Cooking chocolate – 200 gms
Refined oil – 1 tbsp
Chopped walnuts – $1/_2$ cup

Equipment

Ice-cream scoop
Butter paper
Pan
Saucepan
Toothpicks
Butter paper

Use the scooper to scoop
out balls of ice-cream.
Place them on butter
paper and freeze till hard.

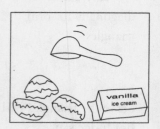

Melt the chocolate in a
pan placed over a pan or
bowl of hot water. Add
1 tbsp of oil to it. Mix till
smooth.

Lift a frozen ball of ice-cream with a toothpick. Pour some hot chocolate over it. Rotate the toothpick so that the whole ball is chocolate coated. Sprinkle some chopped walnuts over it.

Place on a dish lined with butter paper.

Repeat with remaining ice-cream balls. Freeze.

Take out ice-cream bon-bons from the freezer when you wish to serve them.

FRUITY BREAD PUDDING

SERVES—6

Ingredients

Bread – 4 large slices
Almonds – 100 gms (chopped)
Walnuts – 50 gms (chopped)
Sultanas (kishmish) – 100 gms
    (chopped)
Eggs – 4
Sugar – $^3/_4$ cup
Vanilla essence – $^1/_2$ tsp
Milk – 2 cups
Cream – 2 cups

Equipment

Chopping board
Knife
Bowls
Fork
Baking dish
OTG

Cut the bread slices into small squares. Mix chopped nuts and sultanas with them.

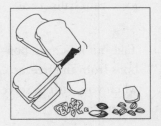

Separate yolks from whites of eggs. Beat yolks with sugar till light and frothy with a fork.

Add yolk-sugar mixture and vanilla essence to the milk in a bowl. Stir well

to mix. Pour in the cream
and mix again.

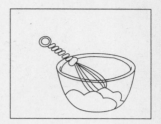

Beat egg whites till stiff.
Fold into the above
mixture.

Butter a baking dish.
Spread the bread-nut
mixture in it. Pour the
egg-cream mixture over
it. Allow it to stand for
30 minutes.

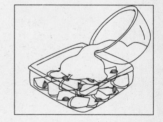

Pre-heat the oven to
180°C. Bake pudding for
20-25 minutes till
pudding is firm and top
lightly browned.

The pudding can be
served hot or cold.